Reptiles

Distributed in Canada by H. B. Fenn and Company Ltd.

Library of Congress Cataloging-in-Publication Data
Weber, Belinda.
Reptiles / Belinda Weber.—1st ed.
p. cm.—(Kingfisher young knowledge)
Includes bibliographical references and index.
1. Reptiles—Juvenile literature. I. Title. II. Series.
QL644.2.W43 2006
597.9—dc22   2005031658

ISBN: 978-0-7534-6177-8

Kingfisher books are available for special promotions and premiums.
For details contact: Director of Special Markets, Holtzbrinck Publishers.

First Paperback American Edition April 2008
First published in hardback in 2006 as *Kingfisher Young Knowledge: Reptiles*
Printed in China
10 9 8 7 6 5 4 3 2 1
1TR/1207/PROSP/RNB(RNB)/140/MA/F

Senior editor: Simon Holland
Coordinating editor: Caitlin Doyle
Designer: Jack Clucas
Cover designer: Poppy Jenkins
Picture manager: Cee Weston-Baker
DTP coordinator: Catherine Hibbert
Production controller: Jessamy Oldfield
Proofreader: Catherine Brereton

Acknowledgments
The publishers would like to thank the following for permission to reproduce their material. Every care has been taken
to trace copyright holders. However, if there have been unintentional omissions or failure to trace copyright holders,
we apologise and will, if informed, endeavor to make corrections in any future edition.
b = bottom, *c* = center, *l* = left, *t* = top, *r* = right

Photographs: *cover* Ingo Arndt/Naturepl.com; 1*bc* Alamy/FLPA/Chris Mattison; 3*bc* Jurgen & Christine Sohns/FLPA; 4–5*c* Corbis/Rod Patterson;
6–7*bl* Getty Images/Marvin E. Newman; 7*t* Getty Images/Jeffrey L. Rotman; 7*crb* Kingfisher/Art Bank; 8*b* Photolibrary.com/OSF/Tui De Roy;
9*tr* Photolibrary.com/OSF/Mark Hamblin; 9*cl* Corbis/Frank Lukasseck; 9*br* Photolibrary.com/OSF/Robin Bush; 10*cl* NHPA/Daniel Heuclin;
10–11*cl* Corbis/Michael & Patricia Fogden; 11*br* Cyril Ruoso/JH Editorial/Minden Pictures/FLPA; 12*bl* Getty Images/Richard Coomber; 12–13*t* Yossi Eshbol/FLPA;
13*b* Heidi & Hans-Juergen Koch/Minden Pictures/FLPA; 14*bl* John Cancalosi/Naturepl.com; 15*t* Corbis/George McCarthy; 15*bl* David Kjaer/Naturepl.com;
16*b* Corbis/John Conrad; 17*t* Getty Images/Peter Weber; 17*cr* Getty Images/Dr. Dennis Kunkel; 17*b* Corbis/Joe McDonald; 18*bl* Photolibrary.com/OSF;
19*tr* Barry Mansell/Naturepl.com; 19*br* Anup Shah/Naturepl.com; 20*b* Corbis/Nigel J. Dennis; 21*t* Getty Images/Paul Chesley; 21*cl* Corbis/ Michael &
Patricia Fogden; 21*c* Alamy/IT Stock Free/Dynamics Graphics Group; 22*bl* Tui De Roy/Minden Pictures/FLPA; 23*cl* Flip Nicklin/Minden Pictures/FLPA; 23*b*
Photolibrary.com/OSF/Tobias Bernhard; 24*c* Pete Oxford/Minden Pictures/FLPA; 25*tr* Photolibrary.com/OSF/Stan Osolinski; 25*cl* NHPA/Stephen Dalton; 25*br*
NHPA/Stephen Dalton; 26*c* Photolibrary.com/OSF/Ingo Arndt; 27*tl* Patricia & Michael Fogden/Minden Pictures/FLPA; 27*cr* NHPA/Daniel Heuclin; 27*br*
Photolibrary.com/OSF/Michael Fogden; 28*b* Photolibrary.com/OSF/Michael Fogden; 29*cl* D. Zingel Eichhorn/FLPA; 29*cr* Rupert Barrington/Naturepl.com;
30*b* Michael & Patricia Fogden/Minden Pictures/FLPA; 31*tr* Getty Images/Steve Winter; 31*br* NHPA/Laurie Campbell; 32*b* Getty Images/Bill Curtsinger;
33*tl* Chris Mattison/FLPA; 33*cr* NHPA/Martin Harvey; 34–35*bc* Corbis/Rod Patterson; 35*tr* Getty Images/Altrendo Nature; 35*br* Getty Images/Theo Allofs;
36*bl* John Cancalosi/Naturepl.com; 37*tr* Photolibrary.com/OSF/Dani Jeske; 37*b* Getty Images/Theo Allofs; 38*bl* NHPA/Anthony Bannister;
38–39*c* Photolibrary.com/OSF/Tobias Bernhard; 39*tr* ZSSD/Minden Pictures/FLPA; 39*br* Getty Images/Joel Sartore; 40*cl* NHPA/Daniel Heuclin;
40*br* Still Pictures/Lynda Richardson; 40–41*c* Corbis/Philip Gould; 48*br* Getty Images/Jeff Hunter.

Commissioned photography on pages 42–47 by Andy Crawford
Project maker and photo shoot coordinator: Jo Connor
Thank you to models Dilvinder Dilan Bhamra, Cherelle Clarke,
Madeleine Roffey, and William Sartin

SCIENCE KIDS

Reptiles

Belinda Weber

KINGFISHER
NEW YORK

Contents

What is a reptile?

Reptiles are a group of animals with tough, scaly skin. They have a skeleton and a backbone. There are more than 6,500 different types of reptiles.

Tough and scaly

Reptile skin is covered in thin, protective plates called scales and is stronger than normal skin. Alligators' skin is covered in thick, horned plates.

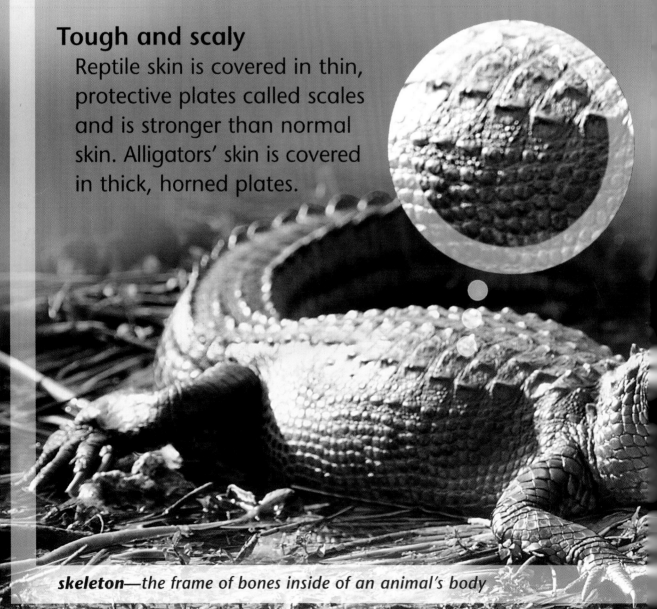

skeleton—*the frame of bones inside of an animal's body*

Water features

Crocodiles live close to water. Like waterbirds, they have webbed feet to help them swim.

Different homes

All reptiles are suited to where they live. Alligators have the correct type of body for moving both in and out of water.

Prehistoric reptiles

Reptiles have prehistoric ancestors. Archelon was a giant sea reptile that is related to modern-day turtles.

ancestor—an animal from which later animals have developed

Different types

Reptiles come in many different shapes and sizes. The largest of all are the saltwater crocodiles, which grow to around 23 feet long. Reptiles are divided into four different groups.

Reptiles with shells

Turtles, terrapins, and tortoises belong to this group. They all have hard, bony shells to protect their soft bodies inside.

species—*a set of animals or plants that have the same features*

Lizards and snakes

This is the largest reptile group. There are more than 3,000 different species of lizards and snakes found all over the world.

The crocodilians

Alligators, crocodiles, caimans, and gharials belong to this group. They can all move quickly on land, but most of them are found wallowing in water.

A group apart

Tuatara are the only members of the smallest reptile group. They are only found on a few small islands off the coast of New Zealand.

allowing—*lying still while floating in water*

Temperature control

Reptiles are cold-blooded, which means that their bodies stay at the same temperature as their surroundings. They lie in the sun to warm up and hide in the shade to cool down. Once they are warm, they hunt for food.

Too cool to move

When some reptiles, such as rattlesnakes, find it too cold, they hibernate (go into a deep sleep) until warmer weather returns.

digest—to break down food so that the body can use it

Staying warm

Chameleons bask in the sun to warm up their blood. Reptiles need to be warm in order to hunt and digest their food.

ooling off

A crocodile cools down by "gaping" its mouth wide-open. Or, it can take a dip in the river or lie in the shade.

Reptile skin

All animals need skin in order to keep their insides in and to stop them from drying out in the sun. Skin also helps protect the animal's insides from injuries.

Spiky skin

Some reptiles, such as iguanas, have spikes along their backs to protect them from predators. These tough scales are made from keratin.

predators—animals that hunt other animal

Smooth skin

Burrowing reptiles, such as sandfish, have smooth, flexible scales. These lie flat against the skin to help the skink slide into its burrow.

Growing bigger

A snake sheds its skin as it grows. It wriggles until it is free from its old skin. This is called sloughing.

eratin—a tough substance found in hair, claws, and fingernails

Reptile senses

Senses help animals understand their surroundings. All animals use their senses to find food, stay safe, and find a mate. Most reptiles can see, hear, and smell, and some can also "taste" things in the air.

eardrum

Listening lizards

Lizards do not have soft ears on the outside of the head like we do. They have an eardrum on each side of their head to pick up sounds

eardrum—a part of the ear that sends sound vibrations to the inner ear

Tasting smells

Many snakes and lizards flick
out their tongue to "taste" the
air. A sense organ in their mouth
figures out what the tastes are.

Looking all around

A chameleon can move
each eye on its own.
This means that the
animal can look in two
different directions at
the same time.

organ—*a part of the body with a special job*

Foot functions

Reptiles exist all over the world, so they need to be able to live in many different habitats. Their feet have evolved and adapted to suit their way of living. Some climb, some dig, while others can grip onto branches.

Spreading the weight

Giant tortoises have huge feet. As they climb over sandy ground, their big feet help spread out their weight so that they do not sink.

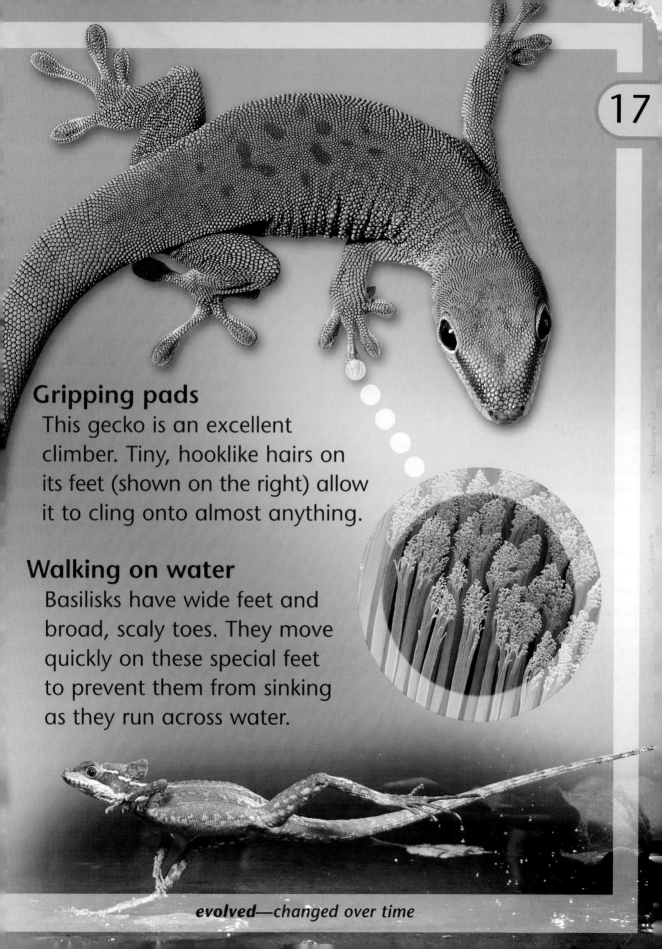

Gripping pads

This gecko is an excellent climber. Tiny, hooklike hairs on its feet (shown on the right) allow it to cling onto almost anything.

Walking on water

Basilisks have wide feet and broad, scaly toes. They move quickly on these special feet to prevent them from sinking as they run across water.

evolved—changed over time

Fangs and teeth

Some reptiles are small and hunt insects. Larger ones eat meatier creatures such as mammals. All reptiles have a mouth and teeth that are suited to catching and eating their prey.

Snapping jaws
The jaws of alligator snapping turtles have sharp edges. The turtles snap them shut to slice their prey into bite-size pieces.

mammals—warm-blooded animals that feed their young on milk

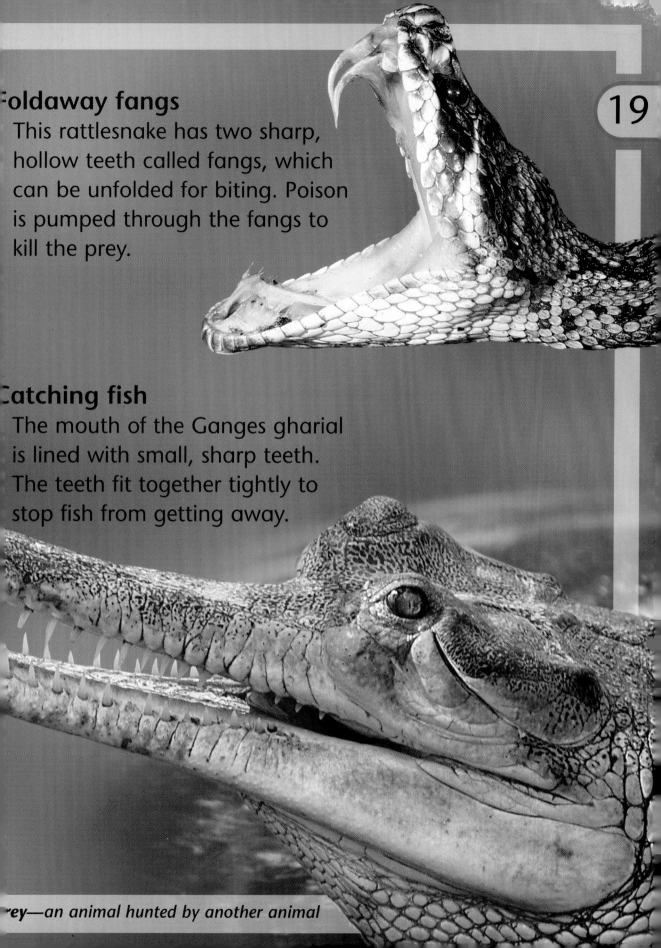

Foldaway fangs

This rattlesnake has two sharp, hollow teeth called fangs, which can be unfolded for biting. Poison is pumped through the fangs to kill the prey.

Catching fish

The mouth of the Ganges gharial is lined with small, sharp teeth. The teeth fit together tightly to stop fish from getting away.

rey—an animal hunted by another animal

Moving **on land**

All reptiles have a bony skeleton that helps give their body its shape. Many reptiles have four legs, but snakes and some lizards do not have any legs at all. Most reptiles can move quickly to hunt or escape from danger.

Handling the heat

The Namib sand gecko has long legs. When it gets too hot, the gecko pushes up on its legs to lift its underside away from the scorching desert sands.

flexible—bendable, stretchy

Sidewinders

Sidewinder rattlesnakes wriggle and loop their bodies along the hot ground. This way, only a small part of their body touches the scorching hot sand at a time.

Inside of a snake

A snake's skeleton has a flexible backbone with ribs attached to it. It is very bendable, so a snake can coil up or wrap around things.

Moving in water

Some reptiles live in the water, while others swim in order to find food or cool themselves down. All reptiles breathe air, so even those that live in the water need to surface often to breathe air.

Finding food

Marine iguanas are the only ocean lizards in the world. They feed on seaweed and can stay underwater for around 20 minutes.

Graceful swimmers

Green sea turtles beat their front flippers like wings and use their back flippers for steering. Their smooth shells help them move through the water.

Powerful swimmers

Saltwater crocodiles swish their long tails from side to side to push them through the water. Their legs help them steer.

flippers—limbs that are suited to swimming

Moving in trees

Many reptiles are good climbers. Geckos that live in trees have special foot pads for gripping slippery leaves, while some snakes have ridged scales for clinging onto branches.

Clinging on

Tree snakes have long, strong bodies. They wrap themselves around branches and reach out into the open to look for predators or prey.

glide—*to gently float through the air*

Gripping claws

Monitor lizards
have strong legs
and feet with long
claws for gripping.

Leaping lizards

The flying gecko has
webbed feet and folds of
skin along its sides, legs,
and tail. It uses these to
catch the air and glide.

Flying lizards

This flying dragon lizard
has flaps of skin along its
ribs, which are useful as
"wings" for gliding.

Finding food

Although some lizards only eat plants, most reptiles are carnivores that hunt other animals. Some reptiles, such as crocodiles, have a varied diet, while others only eat one type of food.

Elastic tongue

Chameleons grip onto branches. They have a long, sticky tongue, which they shoot out at high speeds to catch any bugs that they see.

carnivores—*animals that eat meat*

Eating frogs' eggs

When the cat-eyed snake
finds a cluster of frogs' eggs,
it slurps up the whole
sticky mass.

Leafy dinner

The Solomon Islands
skink is strictly a plant
eater. It climbs trees
to feast on the fresh
green leaves.

resh eggs

The African egg-eating snake
swallows whole eggs. It
pierces the shell in its
throat, so that it
does not spill.

pierce—to prick and break into

Finding a mate

When animals are ready to breed, they find a mate. Some reptiles use smell to attract a partner, while others use colors, sounds, and even dancing. Many males fight to win a female.

Bright throat

This male anole puffs up its colorful throat and nods its head up and down. This shows females that he is ready to mate and warns off any rival males.

breed—to produce babies

Breeding dance

Speckled rattlesnake males prove their strength by wrestling. They are venomous, but they do not bite each other.

Wrestling match

Using their tails for support, male monitor lizards rear up on their back legs and fight rival males. The weaker male gives up.

Reptile eggs

Most reptiles lay eggs with soft but tough shells. The egg's yolk provides the developing young with food. The shell protects it from outside conditions.

developing—*growing and changing*

turtle's nest

This olive ridley sea turtle is laying around 100 eggs into a hole that she has dug in the sand. She will return to the sea after burying them.

Breaking out

Developing snakes grow an "egg tooth" on the tip of their upper jaw. They use this to pierce the eggshell when they are ready to hatch.

Live babies

Some snakes and lizards give birth to live young. This lizard's Arctic home is too cold for eggs.

atch—to break out of an egg

Growing up

Baby reptiles usually look like smaller versions of their parents. They are able to catch their own food as soon as they hatch. Some begin by eating smaller prey than the adults eat.

Digging for freedom
Newly hatched olive ridley sea turtles dig their way out of their sandy nests. They crawl as quickly as they can toward the sea.

miniature—tiny

Growth ridges

As a tortoise's shell grows, another ridge is added to the patterns. People can figure out the animal's age by counting the ridges.

ridges

Caring mothers

Although it is a fierce predator, this female Nile crocodile is also a caring mother. She gently scoops her babies into her mouth to keep them safe.

dge—*a narrow, raised area on a flat surface*

Staying safe

Reptiles use many different tricks to stay hidden while they are hunting or resting. If they are startled, some pretend to be dead. Others show that they are poisonous by their bright colors.

Armor plating

An armadillo lizard has sharp, spiny growths on its skin. When the lizard is threatened, it grabs its tail and curls up into a spiky ball.

startled—surprised

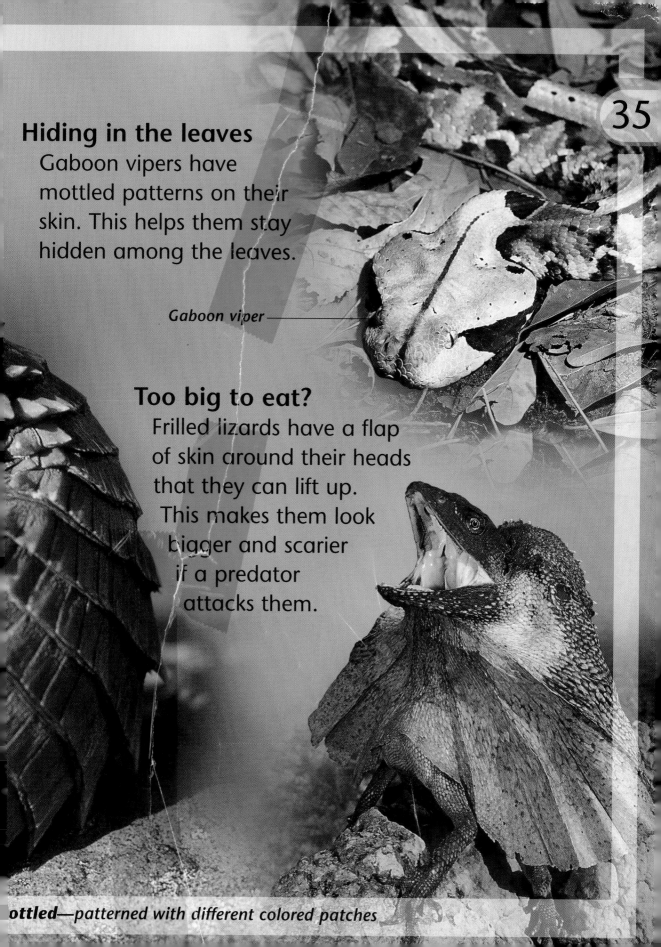

Hiding in the leaves

Gaboon vipers have mottled patterns on their skin. This helps them stay hidden among the leaves.

Gaboon viper —————

Too big to eat?

Frilled lizards have a flap of skin around their heads that they can lift up. This makes them look bigger and scarier if a predator attacks them.

ottled—*patterned with different colored patches*

Dragons and devils

Lizards are the most successful group of reptiles and live in many different places. Some lizards have developed into big and fierce predators. Others are much smaller and live in trees, or even underground.

Dragons with beards

When it is threatened, the bearded dragon puffs up a spiky flap of skin under its chin. This makes it look too big to eat.

Big dragons

Komodo dragons are the largest of all lizards. They can catch goats and pigs, but they usually eat carrion.

carrion—the dead bodies of animals

Thorny devils

A thorny devil's spines and prickles protect the animal against attacks. They also catch dew for the lizard to drink.

ew—*small drops of water that form on grass and plants during the night*

Many reptiles use venom (poison) to kill their prey. Venom can affect the nervous system, the tissues of the body, or even the blood. Venomous reptiles may also use these poisons for self-defense.

Spitting cobras

A spitting cobra sprays venom out of its mouth and aims for its enemy's eyes. The poison is very painful and can cause blindness.

nervous system—the network of nerves throughout an animal's body

A poisonous bite

Gila monsters are
one of two species of
venomous lizards. Their
venomous saliva (spit)
poisons prey as they
bite and chew.

Swimming snakes

Sea snakes are the most
venomous snakes in the
world. They can swim
underwater for up
to five hours.

Noisy rattles

Rattlesnakes twitch the
loose scales at the end
of their tail to make
a rattling sound. This
warns enemies that
their bite is
poisonous.

saliva—clear liquid produced in the mouth

A future for reptiles

Many reptiles are in danger or face extinction. We need to learn how our actions may harm reptiles and do more to take care of them.

Harmful trade

Many reptiles are killed for their skins. The skins are then used to make wallets, boots, belts, and souvenirs for tourists.

Tracking reptiles

This loggerhead turtle is being fitted with a radio transmitter. Scientists will monitor its movements so that they can learn more about this creature.

extinction—when all animals of a certain type die and none are left

Returning to the wild

This alligator was once caught and sold as a pet. Luckily, it was rescued and returned to its real home.

radio transmitter—a device that sends out signals to be tracked

Lizard cape

Make your own frilled cape
The Australian frilled lizard defends itself by using its neck frill (see p. 35). Make one yourself to see how this special defensive system works.

1

Draw one half of the frill shape onto a large sheet of colored cardboard. Use scissors to cut out the shape.

You will need
- Two large sheets of cardboard
- Pencil
- Scissors
- Tape
- Poster paints
- Paintbrush
- Colored tissue paper
- Glue
- String

2

Make the other half of the frill with another sheet of cardboard. Fold each half like an accordian.

3

Place the two halves together and connect them using tape at one end.

Create a pattern for your cape using paint. Cut out pieces of tissue paper and stick them on using glue to create a scaly texture.

Cut two long pieces of string. Attach them at each end of the cape—to the unpainted side—using tape.

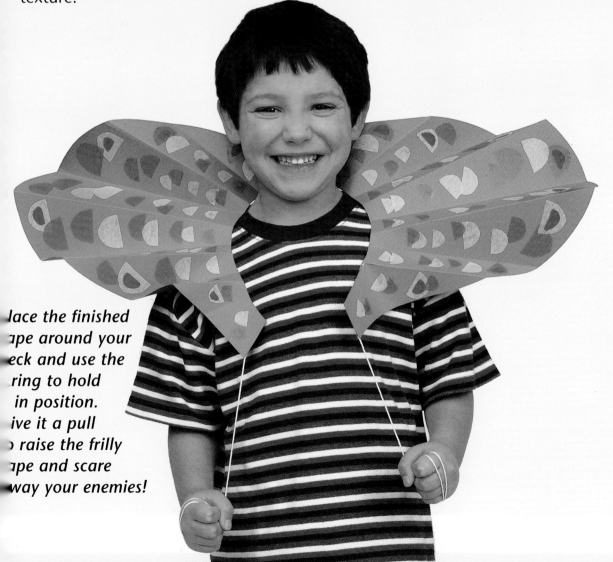

Place the finished cape around your neck and use the string to hold in position. Give it a pull to raise the frilly cape and scare away your enemies!

Pop-up croc

Create a greeting card
Learn how to cut and fold paper to make your very own pop-up card. Then decorate it for a friend or relative.

You will need
- Colored cardboard
- Pencil
- Scissors
- Poster paints and paintbrush

1

Fold the cardboard in half and draw a zigzag line for the teeth. Cut along the line using scissors.

2

Fold the teeth shape out, as shown, so that there is a definite crease. Unfold the cardboard so that it is flat.

3

Draw out the rest of your croc in pencil and color it in with paints. Press out the teeth to make the cardboard work.

Snake stick

Make a slinky snake toy

Snakes have a flexible backbone.
Create this model, then use the
stick to copy the way that a
snake coils and slinks over land.

Use a ruler to draw equal strips
onto the colored cardboard. Use
scissors to cut out the strips.

You will need
- Colored cardboard
- Pencil
- Ruler
- Scissors
- Tape
- Paints
- Paintbrush
- String
- Wooden stick

Using tape, make one strip into a
loop. Connect the other strips on in
loops. Add a pointed loop for the tail.

Add eyes and a forked tongue. Paint
on markings. Stick one end of string
close to the head and the other end
to a stick.

Sticky tongues

Pretend to be a chameleon

Chameleons shoot out their sticky tongues to snatch juicy bugs (see p. 26). With this game, you can pretend to do the same!

Roll up sheets of cardboard to make two tubes—one slightly thinner. Attach the tubes using tape. Paint the tubes red.

You will need
- Colored cardboard
- Tape
- Poster paints
- Paintbrush
- Red tissue paper
- Double-sided tape
- Black tissue paper
- White tissue paper
- Scissors

Fit the slightly thinner tube inside of the larger one. Use tape to hold the two tubes together.

Scrunch up lots of red tissue paper into a ball. Add strips of double-sided tape to make it sticky.

4

5

Push the ball of tissue paper into the end of the long tube. The double-sided tape should hold it in. This forms the tip of your sticky tongue.

Make flies by scrunching up smaller pieces of black tissue paper. Cut out wing shapes using white paper or tissue. Stick them on using tape.

Make two of these sticky tongues. Then, put all your flies into a bowl or onto a paper plate, and you are ready to play . . . The person who collects the most flies in one minute is the winning chameleon!

Index